Sunbather

poems by

Sylvia Dziewałtowska

Finishing Line Press
Georgetown, Kentucky

Sunbather

Copyright © 2024 by Sylvia Dziewałtowska
ISBN 979-8-88838-424-4 First Edition
All rights reserved under International and Pan-American Copyright Conventions. No part of this book may be reproduced in any manner whatsoever without written permission from the publisher, except in the case of brief quotations embodied in critical articles and reviews.

ACKNOWLEDGMENTS

A few references to note:

Pale blue surface of everything—Quinn Latimer
Saute Ma Ville—Chantal Ackerman
In my house I collaborate with whomever I want—Pedro Almodovar
Mother of black-winged dreams—Euripides
So swift, as this, is love—Ovid
Flower or blood—Pablo Neruda
I know what I did and I wasn't thinking of myself, anymore—Reality Winner

I would also like to acknowledge the influence that Walter Benjamin, Max Ritvo, Sophie Calle, Samuel Beckett, Morse Peckham, and Rudolph Arnheim had on particular poems.

This book would not have been possible without my family, friends, mentors, and the Tongva land where I grew up.

Publisher: Leah Huete de Maines
Editor: Christen Kincaid
Cover Art and Design: Jam Yoo

Order online: www.finishinglinepress.com
also available on amazon.com

Author inquiries and mail orders:
Finishing Line Press
PO Box 1626
Georgetown, Kentucky 40324
USA

Contents

Labor Of Dandelions 1

Mythic Domestic Poetic 2

Saint Francis Of Assisi 3

What Is The Cost Of Seeming 4

All This Was Grassland Once, A Prairie 5

Train 6

They Are So Terribly Thirsty 7

Threshold 8

The Argument 9

Three Feathers 10

The Aim To Fail 11

A Canyon Like A Jaw Forever Asking How To Say It 12

Mothering the Rose 13

Fish, Too, Know How A Sailing Ship Burns 14

Saute Ma Ville 15

Saint Teresa of Avila 16

Outpatient 17

Reef 18

A Moment Before Another 19

The Question Of Peace 20

Apophenia 21

When I Said Time I Meant Body 22

Clarion Hotel 23

Shut As If To Shut Up 24

Material Ideal 25

Victory of Samothrace 26

Sunbather 27

Wife Of Weeds 28

My City 29

The Artist Speaks..30

Pictures of Huron 31

Order Is Not The Absence Of Disorder...32

I Will Set Out 33

The Intruder 34

Eros's Speech 35

Futurism Spring Collection..36

Stream 37

Maker of Forms 38

The Vulture..39

A Living 41

For my family

LABOR OF DANDELIONS

Some flowers
disclose
their own seeds,

come undone
by necessity.
The assassination

was a hoax.
Military actions
drove me

no more than
the miracles
of saints. The songs

of devotion
were plagiarized.
No one sees

their own suicide.
The pearl necklace,
I buried.

The manuscript,
I burned.
Pale parachute,

concentrate
on the scope
of chaos:

one blow
is all it takes
to turn you.

MYTHIC DOMESTIC POETIC

Something ancient stirs inside the day. Ochre hues, cobwebs, the beat of wings.
           The sun is the red eye of the horse.
It forces my composure. My chandelier is made of sugar. I have no past.
              The moths arrive one by one. I catch them like the dead and release.
My eyes persuade a ribbon along the edge of the rocks. I could have missed it
                  but I've been listening. A man casts his line from the dock,
                          reels it back as it starts to rain. I know a destiny
of things. Beyond the dogs, a brush fire slips through wet air like the hair
                of a woman swimming. Alone, everything moves along
two horizons, and I've been singing, of jealousy and belief, reasons and tonight,
          I want to fill each glass
until the mountains ash into the palm of my hand, and I am ready to dive.

SAINT FRANCIS OF ASSISI

They woke in a blow of gold
murky coin poised between palms
a fruit bird between palms braving
the weather a wood bird elided
for the unforeseeable weather
a water a spice bird the eye comes
in gold and comes the point
root of fruit flight wound poised
over feather on water light
blood clot in a stretch sky
to the space inside a shy blue
ambitious bird whose eyes shape
light and shadow light and shadow
stir nobody has seen but birds
ripple rolling as a song a fragrant
wing doing weather a busy bird
nobody believes as they play
they play a sea bird jealous
as fruit romantic as wood
tricky as water alive as the palms
that hold the time turn the time
turn back a blow in gold they woke

WHAT IS THE COST OF SEEING

So you want to live on the bluepale surface of everything.
                It's not nothing, this feeling.
                      There is a rope held taut by every hand as if the statue will sink
                                the world before the world
can draw it up. You know the seafloor where impending shapes
                      pass into inequalities of dark,
          home held ajar by your forgetting its name.
What is the cost of seeming
                          or the particular lack of this hot black night
                  that submits like a man lost
        to the words of another feels in them a kind of lightning,
the startling way dissatisfaction streaks the mouth.

ALL THIS WAS GRASSLAND ONCE, A PRAIRIE

Our neighbors Eleanor and Pete were old enough to know
        wild horses in our backyards. Eleanor nods as she stitches me
    a pillow from her yellowy flowers.
                I hold the doll my parents gave me,
whose round, silent eyes tell me stories
      of what it might mean to be a woman,
          wolves, invaders, giants, and other psychic violence
close behind. With fortitude we'd scale the hills,
   catch our own fish and fry it, and having found my purpose
      in our survival, I cut off half my hair to scare
   all those who thought they knew what I could do.
             Get home before the coyotes eat you,
Eleanor mutters from her pink armchair,
     alien crop circles spinning in her dark Maltese eyes.
   Imagine the untouchable space.
      I cover your face with mine.

TRAIN

I said what I said. The water
was cold and the memory
is. Language almost gets bored with itself.
Tonight I've tripped the dry slat. A cat,
the sprawl.
To have an image of it all on the condition
that it's lost forever. Your shape
laying itself down.
The tracks by the dead lot
I will never finish walking.
Further, further.
See the cement rest.
See the cold cement rest.
There are white spiders in floodlights.
A woman, lips like a leaf.
I'd knot all the rope,
bowline, overhand, or reef.
Kids hoot out their window,
bang pots and pans.
Where did the time go?
Sacked in a word somewhere.
In the after-hell I saw
my soul, my mother's soul,
a guardian angel, a cloud of data
floating above my bed
and when I looked in the mirror
I saw myself at every age.
We all looked pretty much
the same.

THEY ARE SO TERRIBLY THIRSTY

Busted cement, blue sky. It's lovesick weather and he's learning
                        the object permanence of people.
            His job is to hang paintings in hospitals.
      Hyperreal or abstract flowers stacked on his rolling cart. Charity of
instinct, aesthetics to offset anesthetics.
                Red, not too red, but red enough.
Permit him to attend the red of his own show: he applies
                the hooks with gusto. The dying woman
watches. He applies the hooks: what the woman sees when she dies
        depends. Early light advances, hands wilting on the weave,
edges along the eggshell finish
                  and is done. Exhale
on his way to the bank. Blue sky, busted cement. Even the weather transacts.
              If our withholding is all we have (there was heat
                    enfolded in the plush petals) why
      have anything at all. Open, called upon to open into the quiet
                    violence of roots and blooms, to roll
back a hunger for, what: he doesn't know
                the names of any flowers.

THRESHOLD

Dreams, too, are rash around a bone,
if words can make a bone,
pliable, prismatic, architecture
of that possible. What comes comes
as a failure of repetition.
When words are so gutted
light can't hold, the colors tear away
like tender meat
but when words are so packed
they brand like hot iron,
I am the meat.
Words make expert clocks, softer
bullets, historical fictions
embodied by sound.
Words should be broken
like rocks until body remembers
what it is to be animal.
Then, words are the only key
I have to lose, to find, to lose
again, fumbling at a blue door,
always a door, always blue,
between a bed and a grove of citrus.

THE ARGUMENT

I don't remember what else. Of the argument, I don't. Only the intimacy of its intrusion, like this rock that rolled down this white road to Echo Lake. Our crescent path shot off and then I felt something like forgiveness, rise like this, the mountains, their light-clung leisure in his bad leather shoes, bursting through snow, fears of reckless driving stoked by swerves the language took towards some steadier venture than voice, vehicle, rushed into the quiet pine, blue-feathered.

Morning's argument I forgot, knowing only how it leaked the intimacy of our intrusion, burst through quiet pine, blue-feathered. Ours is not a precious vehicle, I could have told him then. Dodging rocks to Echo Lake, the crescent path shot off, blue pine dusted light by his bad leather as fears of reckless driving swerved the language towards silence.

THREE FEATHERS

The pigeon fell from the sky
Rapt, agape
So swift, as this, is love
Velocitas firmitudo
Repeat the action
She crashed
To master original trauma
How hard is it
I am nature, I am
Repeat the action
Her wing shattered
To master the sensation of loss
Repeat the action
She shuddered
In my lap and lived
To master the compulsion
To repeat this
Black and red recital
So swift, as this
So swift, as this

THE AIM TO FAIL

Story hangs around event like severe weather, a threat

Universe shaped like a finger trap

There was a plain invitation to fall, fall in

The way sound falls into the heart

How infinity finds choice in the movement, before nothing

Some incredible pain repeating, this is bliss. This is

I never was too dexterous

A CANYON LIKE A JAW FOREVER ASKING HOW TO SAY IT

I heard a god speak through a man on a bed of hot coals, and felt the world turn.
    I crawled inside you and sat like an owl. Fog snaked to my face.
        Shuttering chaparral. Oak tree, drought, sunshine, and tar.
            Each name a refrain of coming and going through a canyon like a jaw
forever asking how to say it. We walked the winding streets arm in arm.
                A pant of warm air flushed with metals and minerals,
we sat under a southern magnolia. A woman did her laundry. I couldn't speak
    through spangled cascades of cotton and chiffon.
        Choosing felt like stacking bricks,
            linear, heavy, inhibiting. I built small houses
            between your ribs as families blew flowers off the mustard plants
                with the wheels of their cars.
        We danced into the nauseous dawn.
            Cerulean swimming pools lined with Spanish tiles and tropical trees.
        Freeways looped like eels in a basin of expensive water and taste.
When I slept in your underbelly, I dreamt of circular thrash
        pinning me at depth, angels leaning over my hospital bed.
                And when I couldn't run anymore,
I ran through you. Endless rolling, expert seize. Raw skin of it.
        Waking became a simple matter,
            conscious of faint sounds, the city streets
            unwound and mouthing
an obvious prayer, covered in heaven and recurring change of plan.
What can we do but steal from failure, stretch history to a pin? This very moment
                as roads, alight on the familiar.

MOTHERING THE ROSE

Feathers drift over newspaper
soaked in A/C drip.
A person in blue clicks past.
I, too, come upon such stillness
and forget about it.
I have believed in the healing powers
of amnesia more than I have believed
in the power of the line to confess
or any reader to forgive.
On the train, quiet ladies in clean linen
navigate collective responsibility
with the rhetoric of health and sickness.
The economy is in poor shape, etc.
Convincing you of my atheism,
I let the numbers lead me back to my body.
Maybe I'm always gesturing
anxiously at the nature of desire
and comparing it to wi-fi
but there are forces and fibers all around,
entire networks stretching
and sounding. Somewhere
there are tall women
pulling at bladed grasses
the way you tear yourself to sleep.
There, a man crushed inside
industrial machinery walks away
unscathed. Here, ghosts of young girls
gather at the top of the hill.
They give their presentations
to God. I turn to face
a drunk, ugly sea pushing time on it.
How loveable we were all along.

FISH, TOO, KNOW HOW A SAILING SHIP BURNS

Static in my ears absorbs the chimes of coins
                            hitting hardwood floors between my parents.
           I may have been three and thought, this is the way
                an ocean subsumes the ripples of raindrops.
                                      Each note wavers
in isolation, viscous membranes thinning as they expand
        until the micro rhythms calibrate with the whole. Routes of commerce
            dissect the harbor into lines of its utility.
We are doing numbers faster than monotony can waken the body to eternity.
              Fish, too, know how a sailing ship burns.
      Fins trace shapes of tension between past and future, individual and collective.
    Even the sea swells geometric extensions of consciousness.
                  How far can sound travel? I may have been three.
                           A way to say through water,
    I'm not a monster, but I'm not above acting one
                               to get what I need.

SAUTE MA VILLE

A politician saw a white moose in Sweden and I watched the video
Laughter rides in on a breeze, I don't want it at all
Unreal West Texas clouds sweep my feed

Our apples have rotted into vinegar
The fridge, like us, is rank and damaged but not afraid
I always tell the truth but the truth keeps changing

We are not the sakura blossoms waving darkly past the window
Nor the waters shifting like a bad reason
But the sacred bursting of the bottle on cement

I love despite circumstance
Though it is a violent slump, the way you behave
Blunting the folds of my instinct

Here I might admit to you how possessive I can become
A knife in the secret drawer of this card table
Forgetfulness makes a good wife out of me

Your MonteCristo cigar box holds paints in primary colors
This derelict blue suits my derelict hand
A broken ukulele poised on its hip like a Picasso woman brings me joy

Ashen eucalyptus bends over lace
Veins crackled like wildfire, some pastoral error
Defiling small histories

In my house I collaborate with whomever I want
Our garden hosts a dry anger and I almost forgot
I steer the hose like a fireman

SAINT TERESA OF AVILA

Strangers glow like chemicals

    in glass vials

  beneath a roiled sky

      streaked lightning white.

I got what I wanted.

    What I want is more

          heat in various tones

running barefoot on the road.

    Can you hear me?

          What I want is

  to accident the surface

as asphalt's brutal glint

    and the trees the trees

see me as I see them,

    glutted by cloud and bodies

        brimming with prophecy,

    untethered.

OUTPATIENT

Close your eyes as the others push you
out. Wings
held close, closer until the bones
recede. Pure muscle.
Pavement. Eyelid.
There.
The body, splayed. Have never seen
such baldness. The body will not
burn. Trembling ants.
Years pass. A feather, long, grey,
falls from my book,
and I am sorry
for any pain caught in my strange
and certain peace.

REEF

As a mollusk secretes its spiral shell, I learn to tear a hole in time
                                        and stay there. "Where did you go,"
        two people ask me on the same day.
                I want to tell them the unconditional does not exist.
                    Not even deep in the oceans
or far out in space. But I catch myself. The unconditional may be a decision
        made in the right conditions. Like the first organism the sun
                beat into being, the first one to decide
to stretch, to feed, to nurse its young.
                    There may have been something
                          unconditional about that.
            Darwin wrote in his margins that evolution
is structured not so much like a tree, but a coral reef.
                    I absorb through my surfaces, like the mollusk,
and like the mollusk, I've been in love. We've been there for four billion years.

A MOMENT BEFORE ANOTHER

The water glistens like an eye, accumulating green or gold.
                Seaweed, scum, glistening sprawl, a kind of cannibal leisure.

    Mud-blue tarp weighted by rain, moths in staggered fight, lilacs in the plot.
Cattail, duckweed, and raspberry. Between blue-black dragonflies

          perched on thorny stalks
        and a robin's cocked head: exchange.

          Like a feeding duck, I float in last night's dream,
so close and sweet we could slice it with a knife, and eat until it's gone.

THE QUESTION OF PEACE

One time at church, I left, then came back and sat in the hall where I could hear the sermon, pipes, and cars equally. The priest spoke of love. I thought of exile, felt the heat on my shoulders, my eyes on the open slit of the door. They sang "Happy Birthday" and mentioned the time—early. Out in the cool of dark, a big red balloon regaled like a moon in the auto shop window. I later thought of peace as the kind of question I'd like to live inside.

That night, the heater crackled to life around the bed. I tried to scream your name behind a caked throat. I tore free to you, there, me, thrashing around a nightmare of brimstone and smoke. A dream within a dream before I woke to the silence of boundless snow. You slipping booties onto Mo, who also has trouble sitting still. Hot coffee in a red-bellied mug. *The Poetics of Space* by Gaston Bachelard. A candle.

APOPHENIA

she fell
hot as-
phalt racing hands
large
awkward—

O Cosmic Descent

the
sky spit
out

whole world re-
petition of ghost
notes

O Mystical Intersection

the feeling was
one

I felt
I'd lived once
before

O Circular Score—

WHEN I SAID TIME I MEANT BODY

sloughing a low and rocky crust. I meant decay, not association
        sprung wild like the morning papaver sprawled across the West,
a primal scream I have never seen.

                      Then I said time and plunged
through the wrong flower, trembling orange despite drought and document
                                    in the field of the skull

where all things form an indiscriminate whole, like a photograph I saw
        of Antelope Valley ablaze.
                I was lost in the field, a blur on someone else's camera.

I prayed against myself,
        took up arms
                against the optics of poppies.

CLARION HOTEL

I came to see a painting.
I came to see a painting I saw
in a childhood dream:
three shadowed figures I could not see
because I was viewing myself
from their perspective. I never saw
the painting. The painting
saw me. A painting
came to see me.

Space does not contain all that is possible.
Magic is not the illness but it can be the cure.

Euripides fell to his knees on the threshold
cradling Earth in aged hands, mother of
black-winged dreams, take me home.

Memory is a hotel.
The hotel is redundant.
Repeat after me.

SHUT AS IF TO SHUT UP

I followed my compass trying
into an empty hope twisted the lid
shut as if to shut up the mouth
the mouth of the mouth
that never spoke until stop
speaking I found coherence
planted its pieces in the sun trying
not for any type of rebirth but
a limit stop speaking a real
restriction always something
there as if stop speaking it was
the opposite of that it was that
there was no opposition to be
had and haunting this infinity stop
leaking was the distortion trying
of one who can't stop feeding
round and round in their head
it was the opposite of that it was
that there was no epiphany
to be had not knowing what
trying not knowing what
light there was being had

MATERIAL IDEAL

In the gorge of the afternoon
                I watch the sheer white
                              curtains embossed with palm fronds
collect the dirty light that eats
                at the core of everything,
                              throw it spinning against the wall.

There is no word but the repetition of a feeling, the feeling itself
                a distant object, rough and round
            like a rock I could kick farther and farther

even as it flares inside me, the world unfixed and afloat.

        And so I swallow
the packed salt, as if my mind could become clear
                as what feeds it—

                the ancient flats of Salar de Uyuni,
                      heart of capital, eye of a coup

"the world's largest natural mirror" says the woman
                in the video on JetBlue,

                      a gesture to the absolute

                luminescence of the land,
                      strangely harboring
                flamingos.

VICTORY OF SAMOTHRACE

Live in such a way that nothing is set in stone. You were built for this.
    One false wing, the other authentic.
You are always moving and you are always still.
      Two planes that never find common ground, we call an itch.
           Distance irritates a wound
        we call a want, a storm caught in one's wings.
Victory of Samothrace quickens the heart.
              What else? The woman's lost her head.
    On the dawn of World War II, she descends
        the wooden ramp of a shelter outside Paris.
Weather warps the architecture into impossible habits of voice.
        Listen to the drip of dark.
              This is what I mean.
      To reconcile past with future,
  tolerate the absence of structure while feeling the lack of it intensely.
      Make finer and finer distinctions.
            Let it be a kind of language
        when light admitted through the iris of one's privacy
    splits the marbled expectation.

SUNBATHER

When it rains in the hills where I was raised,
    waterfalls stream into the canyon.

        Paths are broken by sagebrush and sandstone, split particles
merging in the creek below, which drains through a small estuary
    into the Santa Monica Bay where surfers huddle, waiting for a swell.

        You were in the water then. I was lost to
    the glossy mathematics of light on liquid,
        a kind of clarity,
        sitting on the shore.

Around this time the skies were turning hazy,
    land choked by drought which welcomed the wildfires through
        our doors, windows, into our home, a proper host, to tear it down.

I may have imagined driving inland, later, through barren fields of potted palms,
    your sunglasses askew because your ears are different sizes,
    wondering why all the signs read CRISIS.

    This was after V.'s death but before I saw her swimming.
A seabird, she slipped through and through until I was her, swimming
    across the pool, and at the end of the pool was you, who said,

This can all end right now.
    A flash of light and a burst of color.

        One day when you are old,
    I will tell you how time is a leaky faucet, and days drip
to satiate a sacred place. Or maybe, how time is heat, the glitter and shine,

and we're still stretched under the sun.

WIFE OF WEEDS

Did you, then? Or were you somehow different?
Jasmine or lily.
Flower or blood.
The carménère, its melody of juices.
The first Spanish colonizers brought vines with them.
Lemon or rose.
Wine smells an awful lot like. Fruit, bashed in and bruised, swarmed by flies. Fruit you bloat until it gushes from your throat like wine.
Flower or blood.
They sing. Was I wrong about you?

MY CITY

Is teeming, positioning ourselves like liquid to protect ourselves from time.
I felt proud when I saw my city in a movie.
This history is the history
of shadow as it holds the hull of logic, wet and changing. My city
has terribly unequal tree canopy. Sunlight and open space become problems
when you can't escape. I felt proud when I saw my city moving.
This history is the history
of shade in my city, and this was before I poured myself out to my city,
before the rising cost, and I felt proud when my city saw me moving.
This history is the history
of what rises in the bright. When surveillance
goes up, a tree comes down. I felt proud when my city saw me in a movie,
before a whole new way of seeing
my city sprung up to me, and we could afford the night.

THE ARTIST SPEAKS

I sent my first and foremost self to follow men I met in the street.
                I told the critics and philosophers I did it
                        to seduce my father. The critics and philosophers
            called it a radically manic maneuver, a bold display
         of feminine dependency. Their experience of my experience became an
                oddly compelling creature, a confusion of identity
and intimacy moving market forces independently.
            One successful man even gave me the diploma I was told I needed
                to practice, successfully. Really, I was bored. I became
                      an artist with a second project. Gathered my selves
              for church where I confessed that the ocean
was right, that I was nature and all human ideals,
                and it was alright. Then I told the priest I was becoming
a moth. The priest yawned, so I kept feeding, move after move,
                seeking for my soul some surprise in redundancy,
splitting cells, superfluous, until I was flying on designs of their wanting.

PICTURES OF HURON

We jumped into the river,
Two bright flags plunged in Miro's electric blue.

What is the compulsion between events?

I'd show you how the truth could cease to be
The whole truth, when I jumped
Through your ghost and it laughed.

I'd show you the water darkening,
How it compels you to become
The whole world again.

ORDER IS NOT THE ABSENCE OF DISORDER

A high white sun, black and purple near its center.
        That we might bruise our source to move our source

  is not so unusual. I was a sick man
      with nothing to change into.

I was an eternal circle, a repeated and invariable number
      of coordinated maneuvers executed by commercial grace.

    I was slipping on tensions
      between the world's largest economies,

     a core of iron and nickel, military muscle on a bed of salt.
I know what I did and I wasn't thinking

of myself, anymore, the whistleblower told the FBI agents
      as they searched her home.

  The crowd is waving but the crowd is not a flag.
      Take action today, our sacred light censored,

        our bodies a protest against having one.
 Necessity may look like an accident,

    honesty like a pretty hard game of pretend.
      There are movements of the mind

    playing out in the street, in puddles,
under oaks, circling corporate real estate like traffic.

I WILL SET OUT

The bat swooped low
by my head.
I am the wild animal

you think I am,
walking between mirrors.
Shame is an imaginary thing,

and muscular.
Remember the analyst
who said, in death,

in literal death,
she saw herself released
in the form of giant bats,

a notorious mob, an aurora
of bats. Oh, I will set out
a bowl of fruit

before you tell me
this would be
the right thing to do.

THE INTRUDER

I keep finding myself
in this pink house
wanting to rearrange all
the furniture, but I never
get far—I'm paranoid
that this is not my home.
I am an intruder.

Paranoia is when
the small shoots up
around you like grass.
Paranoia is too smart,
the ultimate confusion.

You would make
a good actress, he says
to me, your emotions
show right on your face.

I grow paranoid
that I've revealed
my disdain for the old
man. I might be eight.

All my life I am
encrypting myself
even as it takes over,
even as I actively
create it, and to think
that you can see it
washing over
my face.

EROS'S SPEECH

    Last night on my front stoop, a stranger approached, introduced themselves as Eros. They spoke of language's capacity to expand the moment; what if we were to call our encounter a "picnic," how would that change it? And a levity broke over us, it's true.

    They said that each moment is a blank slate, that the Greek gods are associated with each finger attached to the hands through which we gesture, make mistakes. I felt a luminous sense of depth compressed into the present, its physicality, as we participated.

    Then came the thought of eternal life, the terror of living it—raw nerves with a skin of cellophane, shored up against some intuition of the infinite—

    In my sleep, boys in uniform climb a wall of wooden hands. I cross out boys and write MEN. One proposes with a toe ring, but not to me. A black cat slinks across the tiles like the one that will soon live alongside me. Then the bull kills me. Dispose of the bull, orders my soul floating above my hospital bed.

    A ghost, maybe V., wraps her arms around the naked soul, whispers in my living ear,

    Cat means eros and apology in dream.

A pine branch sways.
There are the birds.

FUTURISM SPRING COLLECTION

You want to buy a suit, you say.

You like Ralph Lauren uptown, Dolce and Gabbana a block down.

When you say *affection*, I think of poetry, liquid

currency, what we inherit and how we abrade.

I turn gossip into a literary form while you plot revenge;

count your pushups like spare change and drink champagne.

The way you cut into the microseconds, the whole day's a Teycan racing video.

Cool weather, software of the long road

dotted with signs like BLISS and GAIN.

Radio blue-boned crash of night.

Copper glow of the deli sign like so many pennies streaming.

Tomorrow I will commit to every direction,

participate joyfully in my sorrows, incorporate.

I will tell you not to worry,

water always finds its level. Our minds' resources

are flowing into our bodies

and even my pothos is looking pumped, exceptionally vital.

STREAM

The camera stutters traumatic
Light on all their faces.

Matted, aware, wondering
Up new forms of control, they were

Nauseous and known.
What will sink in?

Today, the whir of the fan, the impermanent
Arrangement around sounds I am not.

I forgot what I came here for.
A grid of nails to catch the dead man.

Million-dollar words.
A way to articulate all you have done to me.

Affirming desperations like
I am good and the world is, too.

I am limited in the sense
That an instrument measures

What it was built to measure
And the act of observation

Skews the remark.
How when you tell me

My eyes look a little hard today,
I see a stream running over rocks.

The stream is soft.
The stream is whatever I want.

MAKER OF FORMS

That it can and therefore does alter your curvature,
emotional hazards an invitation
to cross. Call it a pome.
A fruit made of a fleshy, plump receptacle
and a tough core containing seeds.
Call it an apple
by its thin red skin, of the rose family, past tense of rise,
to ascend, to flame, go up in.
So. Beneath a pale sun,
two trees, one of apple, one of fire.
Here, half-light rivers the gut. Between two trees, a mountain
of red sand. What slippage
we choose to scale.
Not to name limits, finitude.
Not to extract. When the entire town is green, the birds
will return, having lost nothing. We will dismantle
our instruments and hold carefully
each glowing grain,
one foot on land, one in water.
To fall in love with uncertainty, this is what we must do.
To become for you a source of
many ways to speak.

THE VULTURE

Lindens everywhere
Deep rooted, crazy
Berries spinning

I am nobody's
Hot pink
Disaster

I am the force
That you are
After

I hope I like
The way you want
Me in my green

Everything is
In or out
Little knobs of heaven

Say something to
Intrigue
So I can get it

Down
Now we have a hot
Pink baby

Our mattress, a single
Spring, our cupboard
A can of string

Beans I eat
Our love, a tiny
Cactus in the vastest

Desert dream
I am the vulture
Dissecting a cloud

When you tell me
It's time
I am the sound

A LIVING

A hitchhiker I offered to drive deep into the Valley told me my name should be Crystal—I'm so clear—after I nearly killed him.

The man works here in Bel Air sanding the insides of jacuzzies. "All you need is a well sanded jacuzzi and traffic that sounds like waves," I recited with a chuckle. He mumbled something about "a living."

When I looked at my cell phone he brought up shellfish, gift of the sea. My Cartier watch glittered like the pale surface of Stone Canyon Reservoir. I asked if my passenger was a poet because I suddenly felt selfish. He said yes, his poems are private and successful.

After we crossed the West Gate onto Sunset Boulevard, my passenger said he could smell souls. When I asked what mine smelled like he sniffed. "Dog. Wet dog."

That night I was reborn with her soul. I groped ahead, aside, and behind on all fours as the mattress shrank beneath me. She.

We. A hybrid organism in the emergent tessellation of a Rubik's cube submerged in the always-dark of the hell-womb.

Forever I woke. The neighbor-dog winked at me. Everything smelled too clean.

When I held the clay imprint of my dead dog's paw print over my heart, something I'd never done before, my pulse thumped wildly.

Her photo stared at me from the bedside shelf, issuing a *Go forth, you'll see.*

I go forth, to the fridge. I see, out the window, a squirrel. I eat kale with my face. I lap kombucha. I chop my hair off because it's hot out.

I love the dead dog inside me. We take a walk around the block. Hear the mechanical clink of sprinklers amidst the "Drought of the Century." See the gardeners clipping topiary in August sun, Mrs. Croft peering through her curtains. Smell the wealth of waste seeping from black bins, the diamonds dripping from exhaust pipes.

Beyond the slope, the country club golf course fans itself in waves of immaculate green, pumping ungodly quantities of water from Stone Canyon. The watch-face glares in the light.

Sylvia Dziewałtowska is a writer from Los Angeles living and working in New York. Her poems and essays have appeared in *BOMB, Bookforum, the Los Angeles Review of Books, No Dear Mag, Harp & Altar, Meridian,* and elsewhere. She is a graduate of the Columbia University Writing Program in poetry.

www.ingramcontent.com/pod-product-compliance
Lightning Source LLC
Chambersburg PA
CBHW020343170426
43200CB00006B/490